B is for Big Sky Country

A Montana Alphabet

Written by Sneed B. Collard III and Illustrated by Joanna Yardley

Photo of Charles M. Russell at his studio easel, courtesy of the C. M. Russell Museum, Great Falls, Montana. With thanks to Kim Smith.

Additional thanks to Don Spritzer for his careful input and ideas; to my information experts Debbie Cheeks, Jerry Hanson, Jeff Helmer, Ladd Knotek, Robb Leary, Peter Lesica, Gina Loss, Murphy McMahon, Paula Nelson, Marijka Wessner, Warren White, and the helpful people at the Charles Russell Museum and Helena Chamber of Commerce; and last, to my enthusiastic Writer's Group—poets one and all!
—Sneed B. Collard, III

Thanks to: The Myrna Loy Center, Great Falls, Montana; The Montana Historical Society, Helena, Montana; The Carter County Museum, Ekalaka, Montana.
—Joanna Yardley

Sleeping Bear Press
310 North Main Street, Suite 300
Chelsea, MI 48118
www.sleepingbearpress.com
1-800-487-2323

Sleeping Bear Press is an imprint of The Gale Group, Inc.,
a division of Thomson Learning, Inc.

Printed and bound in Canada.

10 9 8 7 6 5 4 3 2 1

Cataloging-in-Publication data on file.
ISBN 1-58536-098-8

For the children of Montana,
May your eyes always shine as bright as our big blue sky.

SNEED

For my native Montanan—Max.

JOANNA

MISSOULA PHLOX

A is for Anaconda,
where copper once was king.
The metal that men made here,
helped our telephones ring.

Gold and silver brought the first waves of white settlers to Montana. Copper kept them here. After the invention of the telephone and the electric light-bulb, demand for copper wiring soared. By the 1880s, the Anaconda Copper Company was the largest producer of copper in the world. Copper ore was mined in Butte, Montana and sent by rail to a smelter in Anaconda. Workers used two and a half million special large tile bricks to build the smelter's giant chimney. Today, the smelter is gone, but the 585-foot-high chimney still towers over the landscape.

A a

When you mention Montana, most people think "Big Sky Country." And it's true—the sky here somehow seems bigger, bluer, and more spectacular than in any other state. Why? Maybe it's because the earth curves more here in the northern part of the United States. More likely, it's simply because our sky stretches over such an abundance of beauty.

B, though, also stands for Montana's state flower, the bitterroot, and one of our most famous animals, the bison. If you want to see plenty of bison, visit the National Bison Range near Moiese and Ravalli. Established in 1908, this National Wildlife Refuge is home to elk, deer, pronghorn, black bear, and of course, bison or "buffalo"—the same animals that used to darken the plains in every direction.

Big Sky Country begins with B—
a nickname tried and true.
Gaze above you to understand,
how a sky can be so grand.

C is for Cutthroat Trout,
a fisherman's true dream.
It hunts in downstream waters,
and lays its eggs upstream.

Montana doesn't have just one official state fish. It has two—the West Slope Cutthroat Trout and the Yellowstone Cutthroat Trout. Cutthroat trout are known for hunting downstream in rivers and lakes and returning to their smaller "birth streams" to spawn. The West Slope Cutthroat played a special role in Montana history. When Lewis and Clark were passing through Great Falls in 1805, they became the first white men to catch and describe a West Slope Cutthroat. Today, the scientific name of the fish—*Oncorhynhcus clarki lewisi*—honors these two great explorers (*also see P*). Unfortunately, the past two centuries have not been kind to either of our state fish. Cutthroat numbers have plummeted because of water pollution, dams along Montana's rivers, and the introduction of non-native fish species. State agencies and conservation groups are working together to try to save these beautiful, "fishy" parts of our state's heritage.

Ranchers and scientists have discovered many dinosaur skeletons in Montana—including numerous *Tyrannosaurus rexes*. In a place called Egg Mountain near Choteau, paleontologist Jack Horner discovered the first ancient dinosaur eggs and nests ever found. Some of these nests belonged to *Maiasaura peeblesorum*, a kind of duck-billed dinosaur. This dinosaur nested in large colonies and probably traveled in herds. In 1985, after receiving a petition signed by 8,574 school students, the Montana State Legislature proclaimed *Maiasaura peeblesorum* our official state fossil.

D is for Duck-billed Dinosaurs,
that traveled in large herds.
They had their young by laying eggs,
just like our feathered birds.

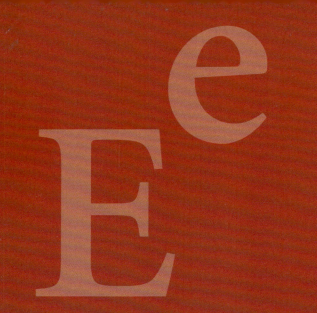

E e

The town of Ekalaka began when the wagon team of Claude Carter, a buffalo hunter, got tired of pulling its wagon full of logs. Carter had intended to build a saloon in gold country farther to the west. But when his horse team bogged down, he decided to use the logs to build a saloon right where he stood. Cowboys, then homesteaders, came to his establishment. The first homesteader was a man named David Russell, who married a niece of the Ogala Sioux chief, Red Cloud. Her name was Ijkalaka and after she and her husband settled in the area, the local postmaster named the town after her. Today, tourists visit Ekalaka for its authentic Western main street and the beautiful limestone cliffs and outcrops close by.

E is for Ekalaka—
say that real fast!
Here's a place you should stop and see,
for beauty, stories, and history.

When visitors first arrive in Montana, they are often impressed by how big everything is! Indeed, Montana is America's fourth largest state, enclosing more than 147,000 square miles—the size of New York, Pennsylvania, Massachusetts, Connecticut, Maine, Vermont, and Washington, D.C. put together. Montana is also home to Flathead Lake. At 28 miles long and 7 to 8 miles wide, it is the largest natural freshwater lake in the West.

Ff

F is for big Flathead Lake,
    and because we are Fourth largest state.
Look around, it's no surprise,
    everything here's been "supersized."

G belongs to Glacier,
the most stunning park of all.
Where wolves and bighorns wander,
and bear grass blooms so tall.

Gg

Over millions of years, the upheaval of the Earth and patient scraping of glaciers created the magnificent mountains and valleys of Glacier National Park. Long before white men found it, Glacier served as a spectacular hunting ground for Indians and a home for grizzlies, wolves, bighorn sheep, and mountain goats. In 1910, the U.S. Congress officially created Glacier National Park. In 1932, workers completed the world-famous Going-to-the-Sun Road. The road twists and turns through the park's glacier-carved valleys and carries visitors up past alpine meadows full of glacier lilies, shooting stars, and bear grass. It crosses the Continental Divide at Logan Pass, 6,680 feet above sea level—and as close to the sun as most visitors ever want to get!

H h

Did you say H? That's Helena.
The capital of our land.
See the copper capitol dome?
That's where our government makes its home.

Helena first burst to life in 1864, after four ex-Confederate soldiers discovered gold in a place called Last Chance Gulch. Because of its central location, Helena quickly grew beyond its golden roots to become a major trade center. By the 1880s, Helena reputedly had more millionaires per capita than anywhere else in the country. The city became the territorial capital in 1875 and voters chose it as the state capital in 1894. Construction of the "copper-topped" capitol building—where the state legislature meets—began in 1899 and was completed in 1902. This magnificent building has recently been restored to show off its beautiful design and wealth of original artwork (*also see R*).

Fire has always been an essential part of the Western landscape. Fires clear away old growth and allow forests, prairies, and other ecosystems to renew themselves. In 1910, however, extremely dry weather and gale-force winds produced a deadly inferno of monster proportions. In only a few hours, thousands of smaller fires joined into several large blazes that charred three million acres across northern Idaho and western Montana. More than 85 people died in the inferno, including dozens of firefighters. Smoke from the fires reached New England and even Greenland. The fire—known as "The Big Blowup"—led to many changes in how we manage forests. After 1910, federal and state governments began investing large amounts of money in firefighting crews and equipment, as well as roads and trails into forestlands.

I i

I "burns" for Inferno—
the fires of 1910.
They charred three million acres,
powered by the wind.

Born near Missoula in 1880, Jeannette Rankin leaped into a political career by campaigning for women's right to vote. In 1916, she ran for—and won—Montana's seat in Congress, becoming the first American woman to be elected to national office. She served a second Congressional term from 1941 to 1943. Rankin worked tirelessly for peace, civil rights, and social justice. Her decisions were often controversial. She was the only member of Congress to vote against entering both World Wars I and II. Later, she led a march protesting the Vietnam War. She died in 1973.

Jeannette Rankin starts with J,
a heroine to admire.
She fought for peace and justice,
with commitment and desire.

J j

K k

K's for Spotted Knapweed,
  a plant we can do without.
The next time you come upon it,
  bend down and PULL IT OUT!

Spotted knapweed arrived in North America from Russia and Europe in the late 1800s, probably as seeds mixed in with alfalfa. Today it infests more than five million acres of Montana alone. Like other noxious weeds, spotted knapweed drives out native plants such as our state grass, bluebunch wheatgrass, and our state flower, the bitterroot. It also robs elk, deer, bison, and cattle of grazing lands. Montana's other nasty invaders include leafy spurge, sulfur cinquefoil, oxeye daisy, dalmatian toad-flax, and Canada thistle. We can all fight the spread of these harmful weeds by washing the soles of our shoes before hiking into wild areas and by planting only native plants around our houses. If you see a stray knapweed plant while hiking or walking, do everyone a favor: pull it out and drop it in the nearest garbage can.

One of the most famous battles in U.S. history took place along the Little Bighorn River on June 25, 1876. There, a large force of Sioux and Northern Cheyenne warriors defeated the Army's Seventh Cavalry, commanded by Lieutenant Colonel George Armstrong Custer. Custer had been sent to force the Indians onto reservations they'd been assigned to. The Indians felt that they should be able to live and hunt where they wanted. As Custer's forces attacked, the Indians fought back and killed Custer and 262 of his men. Today the Little Bighorn Battlefield National Monument protects the battle site and honors the brave men on both sides who died in the battle.

L is for Little Bighorn,
a somber place indeed,
    where warriors and soldiers lost their lives
for causes they believed.

Ll

"SACRED
TO THE MEMORY OF
MARK KELLOGG
CORRESPONDENT OF THE
NEW YORK HERALD
AND REPORTER FOR THE
BISMARCK TRIBUNE
WHO FELL HERE WITH
GENERAL CUSTER
JUNE 25TH 1876"

M m

M is for Missoula
where the Montana Grizzlies play.
Music, art, and culture,
are never far away.

No one seems exactly sure what the name "Missoula" means or where it came from. But today, Montana's second-largest city serves as a center for art, music, and theater. Hundreds of writers, artists, actors, and musicians live in Missoula. The "Garden City" also hosts the International Wildlife Film Festival, the Missoula Children's Theater, the Missoula Symphony, the International Choral Festival, and the two-time National Champion University of Montana Grizzlies football team. Want to see the Grizzlies play? Look for the big "M" on Mount Sentinel above the football stadium. If you hike up Waterworks Hill on the north end of town, you might also see our state flower, the bitterroot, and a beautiful pink flower called Missoula phlox—one of our state's rarest and prettiest plants.

N n

Long before Europeans arrived in North America, native peoples lived in what is now Montana. The U.S. government waged war on many Native Americans, or "Indians," and took their lands. Today, about 60,000 Native Americans live in Montana, mostly on seven different reservations. They belong to the tribes of the Northern Cheyenne, Crow, Blackfeet, Salish, Kootenai, Pend d'Oreille, Gros Ventre, Assiniboine, Sioux, Chippewa, Cree, and Little Shell. Each year, the different tribes hold powwows and other events to celebrate their cultures and traditions. Meanwhile, tribal colleges and training programs allow tribe members to build lasting economic futures.

N is for Native Peoples,
from many Indian tribes.
With proud cultures from the past,
they work toward futures firm and fast.

O is *not* for Orcas—
we don't have them here.
        But Otters, Ospreys, and Great Horned Owls,
        abound here every year.

If you want to go whale watching, don't come to Montana! Our nearest ocean lies 400 miles away. That doesn't mean we don't have plenty of wildlife. Otters are just some of the animals that can be seen in our rivers and lakes, and birds of prey—or "raptors"—love Montana's rich hunting grounds. Great horned owls, eagles, and many other raptors can be seen here year-round. Every spring and summer, look for large numbers of ospreys nesting on trees and on telephone and power poles along Montana's rivers and lakes.

Oo

In 1806, Clark climbed a rock,
and proudly carved his name.
Today, it's a place of history,
Pompey's Pillar begins with **P**.

From 1804 to 1806, Meriwether Lewis and William Clark undertook the first American exploration of the upper Missouri River and the Pacific Northwest. During this journey, the two explorers contacted native peoples, made countless maps, and wrote detailed descriptions of the lands that the U.S. had bought with the Louisiana Purchase of 1803. The only obvious trace Lewis and Clark left of their epic journey was in Montana, on a 200-foot-high stone pillar near the Yellowstone River. On July 25, 1806, Clark carved his name in this rock. He named the rock "Pompey's Tower" for their guide Sacajawea's son Baptiste, whom he called "little pomp" or "little chief." Today, "Pompey's Pillar" is a National Monument.

Montana has produced many fine actors including Gary Cooper and the "Queen of the Movies," Myrna Loy. Myrna Adele Williamson was born in Radersburg, Montana in 1905. After moving to Hollywood and changing her name to Myrna Loy, she went on to star in more than 120 movies including *The Best Years of Our Lives*, *The Thin Man*, and *The Bachelor and the Bobby-Soxer*. When she wasn't gracing the silver screen, Myrna campaigned for social justice, literacy, freedom of speech, and religious tolerance. In 1991, she was presented with an Academy Award for her lifetime achievement in film. She died in 1993 and is buried in Helena.

Q q

Q is for "Queen of the Movies"—
the actress Myrna Loy.
Her long string of Hollywood hits
still bring us fun and joy.

In more than 4,000 paintings and sculptures, Charles M. Russell captured the West like no other artist before him. Born in a wealthy family in St. Louis, Missouri, Charlie had little interest in his native state. Instead, he moved to Montana and began sketching and sculpting the Indians, cowboys, wildlife, and scenery around him. In 1911, the State of Montana hired Russell to paint one of his largest and most important works, *Lewis and Clark Meeting Indians at Ross' Hole*. This painting can still be viewed in our state capitol. By the time he died in 1926, Russell's art had become famous throughout the world. Next to his home and studio in Great Falls, a museum now stands—a tribute to the artist and his art.

Rr

R is for Charlie Russell,
a man of many skills.
He captured our state in paint and bronze,
in ways that move us still.

S s

Look in any park, pickup truck, or passenger seat and you'll see that Montana is definitely a "dog state." Of all Montana's dogs past and present, however, Shep is the most honored. In 1936, Shep's owner died and Shep watched as the man's body was placed on a train in Fort Benton and shipped east. For more than five years afterward, through blistering heat and blinding snow, Shep met every incoming train and searched the passengers for his dead master. Shep's vigil ended tragically in 1942, when he slipped and was killed by one of the trains he was waiting to meet. Today, a monument in Fort Benton commemorates the most faithful dog Montana has ever known.

A most loyal Montana dog,
Shep begins with S.
For five sad years he watched the trains,
for the master who never came.

Even though Montana is most often called "Big Sky Country," our official nickname is "The Treasure State." This title undoubtedly sprouted from the gold, silver, and other precious metals discovered here. So did Montana's official motto, "Oro y Plata"—Spanish for "Gold and Silver." Despite our mining past, however, today's Montanans place greater value on our state's other treasures—our forests, mountains, rivers, prairies and, of course, our friendly, hardworking people.

Speaking of treasures, our state tree is the ponderosa pine. Our state gemstones are the sapphire and the moss agate. Yogo sapphires—mined in Yogo Gulch in central Montana—are shipped all over the world and are famous for their clarity and cornflower-blue beauty.

Montana's other treasures are depicted on our state flag. The flag was created for the First Montana Infantry in 1898 and was adopted as the state flag in 1905. The flag features the state seal, which shows off Montana's natural beauty and early industries. The word "Montana" was added to the flag in 1981.

T is for "Treasure State,"
the nickname that we shout.
With our minerals, trees, and wilderness,
it's not hard to figure out!

MONTANA

Tt

Up until the early 1800s, Montana's state animal—the grizzly bear—lived throughout the West. Today, Montana is one of the last strongholds for the bears in the lower 48 states. Adult male grizzly bears can weigh up to 1,000 pounds, though most Montana grizzlies run about half that size. Several hundred grizzlies live in Glacier and Yellowstone National Parks. They feed mostly on berries, seeds, flowers, and other vegetable matter, but will also devour ladybugs, fish, elk, rodents, and about any other prey they can catch. The bears usually leave people alone, but if you see one, take my advice: Get out of the way!

U is for *Ursus arctos horribilis,*
a bear we call "the griz."
With golden fur both thick and sleek,
it climbs Montana's majestic peaks.

V's for Virginia City,
our first official town.
When men discovered gold here,
it turned Montana upside down!

PRODUCE GROCERIES

J.C OREM'S
MELODEON HALL

BREWERY

RESTAURANT

ST CHARLES

OOT SHOE SHOP

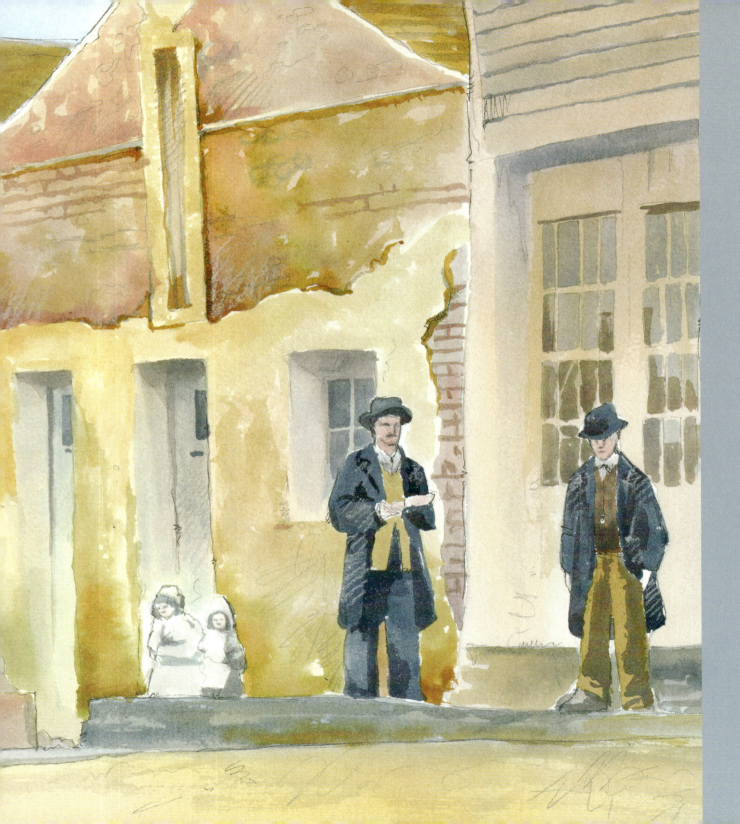

V v

Like Helena—and many other Montana towns—Virginia City got its start when a small group of miners discovered rich deposits of gold here. Word streaked through the region. By 1864—only a year later—18,000 miners and traders had arrived in Virginia City. They lived in a ramshackle assortment of houses, wagons, and tents. Many simply camped out under trees and bushes. Virginia City soon became Montana's first officially incorporated town and boasted the territory's first newspaper, the *Montana Post*. Today, this historical site has been preserved as it used to be and draws thousands of tourists who wish to enjoy some summer theater and explore Montana's colorful past.

As in many other parts of our nation, the wolf was exterminated from Montana more than 60 years ago. Back then, people feared wolves as killers of people, livestock, and wildlife. Since then, we've learned that wolves, people, and livestock can coexist. We've also learned that by eating excess elk and other grazing animals, wolves help protect forests and grasslands. The first wolf returned to Montana from Canada, probably in 1979. Now, wolves can be heard howling in many parts of our state. We're proud to have them back!

Another welcome Montana animal is our state bird, the Western Meadowlark. It can be heard harmonizing from fence posts in most parts of the state.

W "howls" for Wolves,
and also for Welcome Back.
We're glad to see you come back home,
and wander with your packs.

X stands for Xenia,
a forgotten railroad station.
Homesteaders once hurried here
from all across the nation.

In June 1887, the company that would become the Great Northern Railway began building a rail route westward across the northern part of Montana. Work crews built 643 miles of track in seven and a half months—a remarkable feat that has never been equaled. The railroad carried thousands of homestead farmers into this stretch of Montana—now known as the "Hi-line" or "High Line"—and for a few years they prospered. When an extended drought came, however, most of the homesteaders packed up and left. Many stations such as Xenia—between Kremlin and Gildford—were eventually closed and are hardly remembered today.

Y y

Y "runs" for Yellowstone—
the river, not the park.
Its waters flow mostly through our state,
though Wyoming is where they start.

Although its headwaters lie in Yellowstone National Park in Wyoming, the Yellowstone River flows primarily through Montana. Montana's second largest river after the Missouri, the Yellowstone once teamed with wildlife. One early explorer observed a herd of bison along the river that covered 50 square miles! The river basin was a favorite hunting ground for Crow, Sioux, and other Indian tribes. Before the railroad arrived in the 1880s, the river's boat traffic carried people and goods between eastern Montana and the rest of the country. This convenient transportation gave rise to Miles City, Glendive, Sidney, and Montana's largest city, Billings.

Montana's interesting mammals aren't all as big as grizzly bears. In the southeastern corner of the state you'll find a handsome little critter known as the meadow jumping mouse. Like a kangaroo, this long-tailed mouse hops along, grasping insects and grass seeds with its front paws. It may also stop to dig for its favorite fungus to eat. Meadow jumping mice are common in the eastern United States, but Montana is about as far west as they get. Here, they are active from spring to early fall. In winter, they hibernate in deep, protective burrows—a lot like many of Montana's human residents.

Z is for *Zapus hudsonius*,
the meadow jumping mouse.
Don't look for it in winter—
it stays inside its house.

Z z

A Big Sky Full of Facts

1. Which road crosses Glacier National Park?
2. What animal has recently returned to Montana after being exterminated more than 60 years ago?
3. Which Montanan fought for women's right to vote?
4. What is one of Montana's worst weeds?
5. What are three Montana cities where gold was mined?
6. Which Montana actress starred in the movie *The Best Years of Our Lives*?
7. What is Montana's state fossil?
8. When did the Battle of the Little Bighorn take place?
9. Which famous explorer carved his name in Pompey's Pillar?
10. Can you name some of the Indian tribes that live in Montana?
11. What are Montana's two largest rivers?
12. What was the most important metal mined in Butte?
13. What are Montana's *official* nickname and motto?
14. What state fish was named after Lewis and Clark?
15. How many states are bigger than Montana?
16. Which Montana city can you visit to find a lot of art and culture and watch the Montana Grizzlies football team play?
17. Name Montana's most famous—and loyal—dog.

Answers

1. The Going-to-the-Sun Road
2. The wolf
3. Jeannette Rankin
4. Spotted knapweed
5. Butte, Helena, and Virginia City
6. Myrna Loy
7. *Maiasaura peeblesorum*
8. June 25, 1876
9. William Clark
10. Northern Cheyenne, Crow, Blackfeet, Salish, Kootenai, Pend d'Oreille, Gros Ventre, Assiniboine, Sioux, Chippewa, Cree, and Little Shell

11. The Missouri and the Yellowstone
12. Copper
13. "The Treasure State" and "Oro y Plata"
14. The West Slope Cutthroat Trout
15. 3—Alaska, Texas, and California
16. Missoula
17. Shep

Sneed B. Collard III

Sneed B. Collard III has written more than 30 books for young people including the popular titles *Animal Dads, Leaving Home, Beaks!, Butterfly Count,* and *The Forest in the Clouds,* which *Booklist* magazine named one of their Top Ten Children's Science Books and the International Reading Association selected as a Teacher's Choices book. Sneed lives in Missoula, Montana within sight of the giant "M". When he's not writing or walking his border collie, Mattie, he often can be found speaking to school children and teachers around the country about science, nature, and writing.

Joanna Yardley

Joanna Yardley was born in Bishop's Stortford England and moved to the states as a child. She is a graduate of RISD (Rhode Island School of Design) and has had the pleasure of working with some of the greats in the industry—Chris Van Allsburg, David Macaulay, and Jane Yolen. She has illustrated a number of award-winning children's books including *The Bracelet* by Yoshiko Uchida, which was named a *New York Times Book Review* Best Illustrated Book. Jo and her husband Dale have lived on both coasts and now both borders of this beautiful country. They are raising their son Max in Missoula, Montana along with their pets—Osa and Serena.